PIANO | VOCAL | GUITAR

SINGER SONGWRITER
C·O·L·L·E·C·T·I·O·N

Cover Photos:

Joan Baez © Gai Terrell/Redferns/Retna LTD.

Dan Fogelberg © Robb D. Cohen/Retna LTD.

Jackson Browne © Kelly A. Swift/Retna LTD.

Nanci Griffith © Peter Doherty/Retna UK/Retna LTD., USA

Carol King © Steve Rapport/Retna UK/Retna LTD., USA

Leonard Cohen © Sunshine Intern/Retna LTD.

Tom Waits © David Corio/Retna LTD.

Janis Ian © Andrew Kent/Retna LTD.

ISBN: 978-1-4234-5541-7

HAL·LEONARD®
CORPORATION
7777 W. BLUEMOUND RD. P.O. BOX 13819 MILWAUKEE, WI 53213

Visit Hal Leonard Online at
www.halleonard.com

CONTENTS

ALICE'S RESTAURANT

Words and Music by
ARLO GUTHRIE

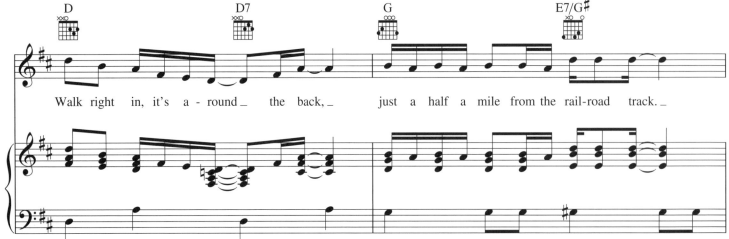

Spoken word: (repeat music from chorus as needed - sing chorus where indicated)
This song is called Alice's Restaurant, and it's about Alice, and the restaurant, but Alice's Restaurant is not the name of the restaurant, that's just the name of the song, and that's why I called the song Alice's Restaurant.

Chorus

Now it all started two Thanksgivings ago, was on - two years ago on Thanksgiving, when my friend and I went up to visit Alice at the restaurant, but Alice doesn't live in the restaurant, she lives in the church nearby the restaurant, in the bell-tower, with her husband Ray and Fasha the dog. And livin' in the bell tower like that, they got a lot of room downstairs where the pews used to be in. Havin' all that room, seein' as how they took out all the pews, they decided that they didn't have to take out their garbage for a long time.

We got up there, we found all the garbage in there, and we decided it'd be a friendly gesture for us to take the garbage down to the city dump. So we took the half a ton of garbage, put it in the back of a red VW microbus, took shovels and rakes and implements of destruction and headed on toward the city dump.

Well we got there and there was a big sign and a chain across the dump saying, "Closed on Thanksgiving." And we had never heard of a dump closed on Thanksgiving before, and with tears in our eyes we drove off into the sunset looking for another place to put the garbage.

We didn't find one. Until we came to a side road, and off the side of the side road there was another fifteen foot cliff and at the bottom of the cliff there was another pile of garbage. And we decided that one big pile is better than two little piles, and rather than bring that one up we decided to throw ours down.

That's what we did, and drove back to the church, had a Thanksgiving dinner that couldn't be beat, went to sleep and didn't get up until the next morning, when we got a phone call from officer Obie. He said, "Kid, we found your name on an envelope at the bottom of a half a ton of garbage, and just wanted to know if you had any information about it." And I said, "Yes, sir, Officer Obie, I cannot tell a lie, I put that envelope under that garbage."

After speaking to Obie for about forty-five minutes on the telephone we finally arrived at the truth of the matter and said that we had to go down and pick up the garbage, and also had to go down and speak to him at the police officer's station. So we got in the red VW microbus with the shovels and rakes and implements of destruction and headed on toward the police officer's station.

Now friends, there was only one or two things that Obie coulda done at the police station, and the first was he could have given us a medal for being so brave and honest on the telephone, which wasn't very likely, and we didn't expect it, and the other thing was he could have bawled us out and told us never to be seen driving garbage around the vicinity again, which is what we expected, but when we got to the police officer's station there was a third possibility that we hadn't even counted upon, and we was both immediately arrested. Handcuffed. And I said "Obie, I don't think I can pick up the garbage with these handcuffs on." He said, "Shut up, kid. Get in the back of the patrol car."

And that's what we did, sat in the back of the patrol car and drove to the quote "Scene of the Crime" unquote. I want tell you about the town of Stockbridge, Massachusetts, where this happened here, they got three stop signs, two police officers, and one police car, but when we got to the Scene of the Crime there was five police officers and three police cars, being the biggest crime of the last fifty years, and everybody wanted to get in the newspaper story about it. And they was using up all kinds of cop equipment that they had hanging around the police officer's station. They was taking plaster tire tracks, foot prints, dog smelling prints, and they took twenty seven eight-by-ten colour glossy photographs with circles and arrows and a paragraph on the back of each one explaining what each one was to be used as evidence against us. Took pictures of the approach, the getaway, the northwest corner the southwest corner and that's not to mention the aerial photography.

After the ordeal, we went back to the jail. Obie said he was going to put us in the cell. Said, "Kid, I'm going to put you in the cell, I want your wallet and your belt." And I said, "Obie, I can understand you wanting my wallet so I don't have any money to spend in the cell, but what do you want my belt for?" And he said, "Kid, we don't want any hangings." I said, "Obie, did you think I was going to hang myself for littering?" Obie said he was just making sure, and friends Obie was, cause he took out the toilet seat so I couldn't hit myself over the head and drown, and he took out the toilet paper so I couldn't bend the bars roll out the - roll the toilet paper out the window, slide down the roll and have an escape. Obie was making sure, and it was about four or five hours later that Alice (remember Alice? It's a song about Alice), Alice came by and with a few nasty words to Obie on the side, bailed us out of jail, and we went back to the church, had another Thanksgiving dinner that couldn't be beat, and didn't get up until the next morning, when we all had to go to court.

We walked in, sat down, Obie came in with the twenty seven eight-by-ten colour glossy pictures with circles and arrows and a paragraph on the back of each one, sat down. Man came in said, "All rise." We all stood up, and Obie stood up with the twenty seven eight-by-ten colour glossy pictures, and the judge walked in sat down with a seeing eye dog, and he sat down, we sat down. Obie looked at the seeing eye dog, and then at the twenty seven eight-by-ten colour glossy pictures with circles and arrows and a paragraph on the back of each one, and looked at the seeing eye dog. And then at twenty seven eight-by-ten colour glossy pictures with circles and arrows and a paragraph on the back of each one and began to cry, 'cause Obie came to the realization that it was a typical case of American blind justice, and there wasn't nothing he could do about it, and the judge wasn't going to look at the twenty seven eight-by-ten colour glossy pictures with the circles and arrows and a paragraph on the back of each one explaining what each one was to be used as evidence against us. And we was fined $50 and had to pick up the garbage in the snow, but thats not what I came to tell you about.

Came to talk about the draft.

They got a building down New York City, it's called Whitehall Street, where you walk in, you get injected, inspected, detected, infected, neglected and selected. I went down to get my physical examination one day, and I walked in, I sat down, got good and drunk the night before, so I looked and felt my best when I went in that morning. `Cause I wanted to look like the all-American kid from New York City, man I wanted, I wanted to feel like the all-, I wanted to be the all-American kid from New York, and I walked in, sat down, I was hung down, brung down, hung up, and all kinds o' mean nasty ugly things. And I walked in and sat down and they gave me a piece of paper, said, "Kid, see the psychiatrist, room 604." And I went up there, I said, "Shrink, I want to kill. I mean, I wanna, I wanna kill. Kill. I wanna, I wanna see, I wanna see blood and gore and guts and veins in my teeth. Eat dead burnt bodies. I mean kill, Kill, KILL, KILL." And I started jumpin up and down yelling, "KILL, KILL," and he started jumpin up and down with me and we was both jumping up and down yelling, "KILL, KILL." And the Sergeant came over, pinned a medal on me, sent me down the hall, said, "You're our boy."

Didn't feel too good about it.

Proceeded on down the hall gettin more injections, inspections, detections, neglections and all kinds of stuff that they was doin' to me at the thing there, and I was there for two hours, three hours, four hours, I was there for a long time going through all kinds of mean nasty ugly things and I was just having a tough time there, and they was inspecting, injecting every single part of me, and they was leaving no part untouched. Proceeded through, and when I finally came to see the last man, I walked in, walked in sat down after a whole big thing there, and I walked up and said, "What do you want?" He said, "Kid, we only got one question. Have you ever been arrested?"

And I proceeded to tell him the story of the Alice's Restaurant Massacre, with full orchestration and five part harmony and stuff like that and all the phenome... - and he stopped me right there and said, "Kid, did you ever go to court?"

And I proceeded to tell him the story of the twenty seven eight-by-ten colour glossy pictures with the circles and arrows and the paragraph on the back of each one, and he stopped me right there and said, "Kid, I want you to go and sit down on that bench that says Group W .... NOW kid!!"

And I, I walked over to the, to the bench there, and there is, Group W's where they put you if you may not be moral enough to join the army after committing your special crime, and there was all kinds of mean nasty ugly looking people on the bench there. Mother rapers. Father stabbers. Father rapers! Father rapers sitting right there on the bench next to me! And they was mean and nasty and ugly and horrible crime-type guys sitting on the bench next to me. And the meanest, ugliest, nastiest one, the meanest father raper of them all, was coming over to me and he was mean 'n' ugly 'n' nasty 'n' horrible and all kind of things and he sat down next to me and said, "Kid, whad'ya get?" I said, "I didn't get nothing, I had to pay $50 and pick up the garbage." He said, "What were you arrested for, kid?" And I said, "Littering." And they all moved away from me on the bench there, and the hairy eyeball and all kinds of mean nasty things, till I said, "And creating a nuisance." And they all came back, shook my hand, and we had a great time on the bench, talkin about crime, mother stabbing, father raping, all kinds of groovy things that we was talking about on the bench. And everything was fine, we was smoking cigarettes and all kinds of things, until the Sergeant came over, had some paper in his hand, held it up and said.

"Kids, this-piece-of-paper's-got-47-words-37-sentences-58-words-we-wanna- know-details-of-the-crime-time-of-the-crime-and-any-other-kind-of-thing- you-gotta-say-pertaining-to-and-about-the-crime-I-want-to-know-arresting- officer's-name-and-any-other-kind-of-thing-you-gotta-say", and talked for forty-five minutes and nobody understood a word that he said, but we had fun filling out the forms and playing with the pencils on the bench there, and I filled out the massacre with the four part harmony, and wrote it down there, just like it was, and everything was fine and I put down the pencil, and I turned over the piece of paper, and there, there on the other side, in the middle of the other side, away from everything else on the other side, in parentheses, capital letters, quotated, read the following words:
"Kid, have you rehabilitated yourself?"

I went over to the Sergeant, said, "Sergeant, you got a lotta damn gall to ask me if I've rehabilitated myself, I mean, I mean, I mean that just, I'm sittin' here on the bench, I mean I'm sittin here on the Group W bench 'cause you want to know if I'm moral enough join the army, burn women, kids, houses and villages after bein' a litterbug." He looked at me and said, "Kid, we don't like your kind, and we're gonna send your fingerprints off to Washington."And friends, somewhere in Washington enshrined in some little folder, is a study in black and white of my fingerprints. And the only reason I'm singing you this song now is cause you may know somebody in a similar situation, or you may be in a similar situation, and if you're in a situation like that there's only one thing you can do and that's walk into the shrink wherever you are, just walk in say "Shrink, You can get anything you want, at Alice's restaurant." And walk out. You know, if one person, just one person does it they may think he's really sick and they won't take him. And if two people, two people do it, in harmony, they may think they're both faggots and they won't take either of them. And three people do it, three, can you imagine, three people walking in singin a bar of Alice's Restaurant and walking out. They may think it's an organization. And can you, can you imagine fifty people a day, I said fifty people a day walking in singin a bar of Alice's Restaurant and walking out. And friends they may thinks it's a movement.

And that's what it is, the Alice's Restaurant Anti-Massacre Movement, and all you got to do to join is sing it the next time it come's around on the guitar.With feeling. So we'll wait for it to come around on the guitar, here and sing it when it does. Here it comes.

Chorus

That was horrible. If you want to end war and stuff you got to sing loud. I've been singing this song now for twenty five minutes. I could sing it for another twenty five minutes. I'm not proud... or tired.So we'll wait till it comes around again, and this time with four part harmony and feeling.We're just waitin' for it to come around is what we're doing. All right now.

Chorus, take final ending

AMERICAN PIE

Words and Music by
DON McLEAN

A long, long time a-go I can still re-mem-ber how that

mu-sic used to make me smile. _____ And

I knew if I had my chance that I could make those peo-ple dance and

day the mu - sic died. And they were sing - in'

CODA

this - 'll be the day ___ that I ___ die. ___

Additional Lyrics

2. Now for ten years we've been on our own,
   And moss grows fat on a rollin' stone
   But that's not how it used to be
   When the jester sang for the king and queen
   In a coat he borrowed from James Dean
   And a voice that came from you and me
   Oh and while the king was looking down,
   The jester stole his thorny crown
   The courtroom was adjourned,
   No verdict was returned
   And while Lenin read a book on Marx
   The quartet practiced in the park
   And we sang dirges in the dark
   The day the music died
   We were singin'...bye-bye... etc.

3. Helter-skelter in the summer swelter
   The birds flew off with a fallout shelter
   Eight miles high and fallin' fast,
   It landed foul on the grass
   The players tried for a forward pass,
   With the jester on the sidelines in a cast
   Now the half-time air was sweet perfume
   While the sergeants played a marching tune
   We all got up to dance
   But we never got the chance
   'Cause the players tried to take the field,
   The marching band refused to yield
   Do you recall what was revealed
   The day the music died
   We started singin'... bye-bye...etc.

4. And there we were all in one place,
   A generation lost in space
   With no time left to start again
   So come on, Jack be nimble, Jack be quick,
   Jack Flash sat on a candlestick
   'Cause fire is the devil's only friend
   And as I watched him on the stage
   My hands were clenched in fits of rage
   No angel born in hell
   Could break that Satan's spell
   And as the flames climbed high into the night
   To light the sacrificial rite
   I saw Satan laughing with delight
   The day the music died
   He was singin'...bye-bye...etc.

AND WHEN I DIE

Words and Music by
LAURA NYRO

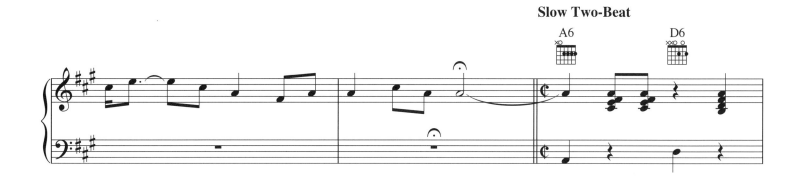

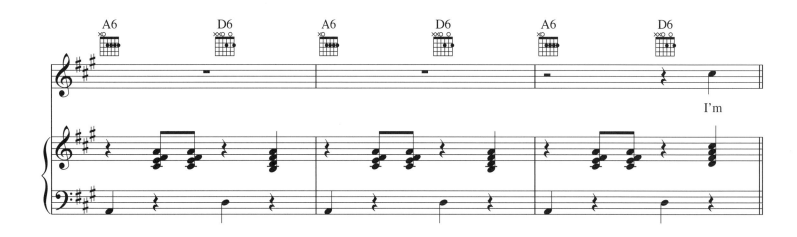

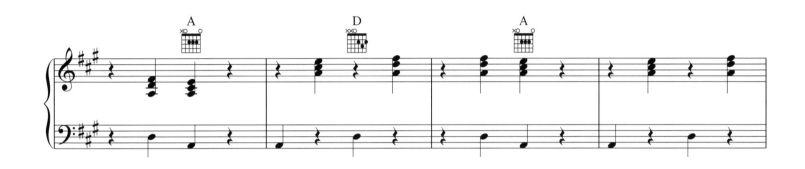

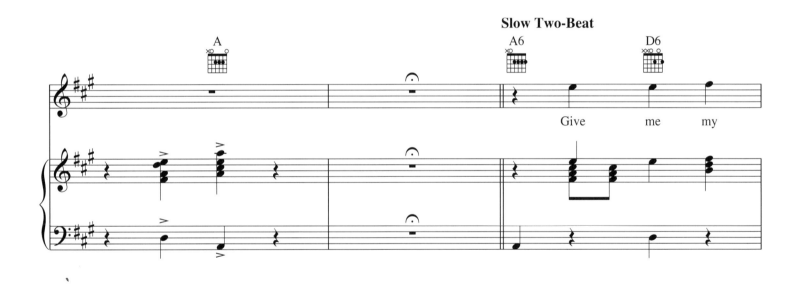

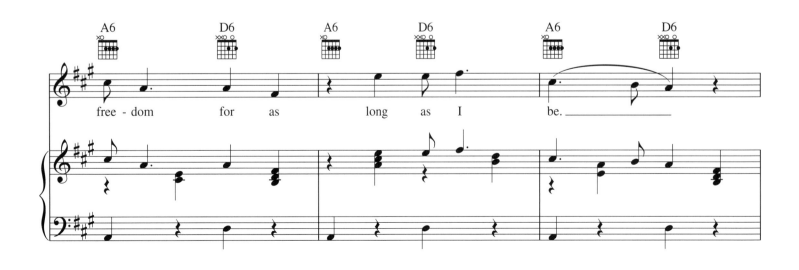

Half tempo Rock

and when I'm dead, dead and gone, _____ there'll be one child

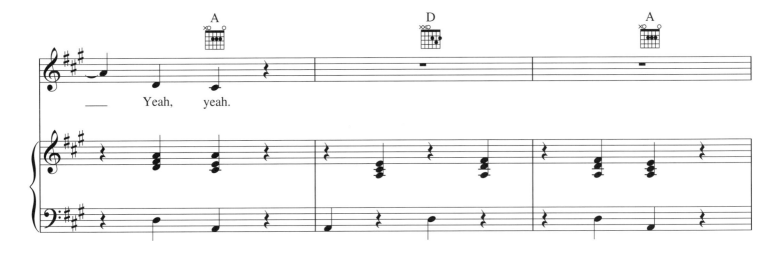

Fast

born in our world to car - ry on, to car - ry on. _____

_____ Yeah, yeah.

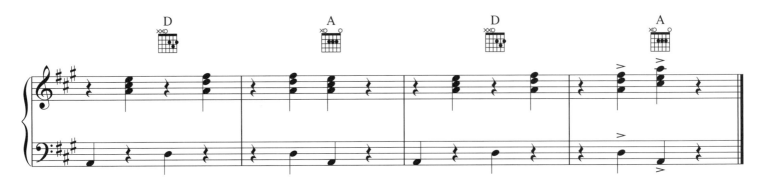

BY THE TIME I GET TO PHOENIX

Words and Music by
JIMMY WEBB

ANTICIPATION

Words and Music by
CARLY SIMON

AT SEVENTEEN

Words and Music by
JANIS IAN

BABY DON'T GET HOOKED ON ME

Words and Music by
MAC DAVIS

Girl, you're get-tin' that
Girl, you're a hot-blood-ed

look in your eyes; and it's start-ing to wor-ry me.
wom-an, child, and it's warm where you're touch-ing me.

I ain't read-y for no fam-i-ly ties;
But I can tell by your trem-bl-in' smile;

hooked on me._____ 'Cause I'll just use___ you, then I'll

set you free._____ Ba - by, ba - by, don't___ get

hooked on me.____

Repeat and Fade

BLOWIN' IN THE WIND

Words and Music by
BOB DYLAN

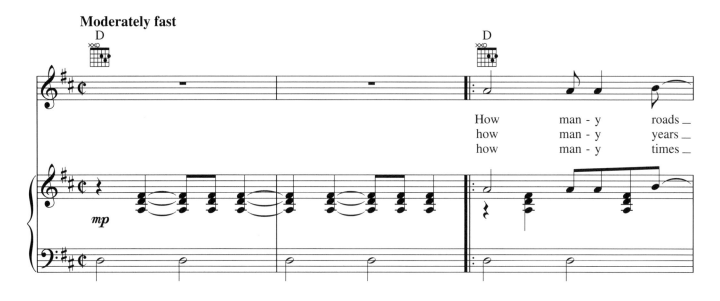

How man-y roads __
how man-y years __
how man-y times __

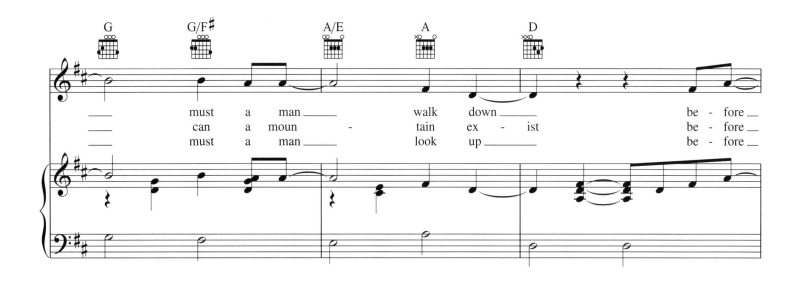

__ must a man __ walk down __ be - fore __
__ can a moun - tain ex - ist __ be - fore __
__ must a man __ look up __ be - fore __

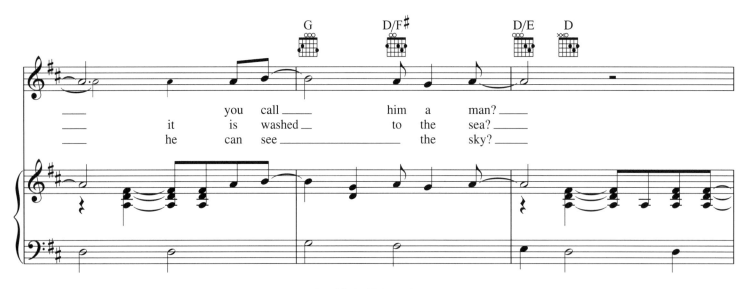

__ you call __ him a man? __
__ it is washed __ to the sea? __
__ he can see __ the sky? __

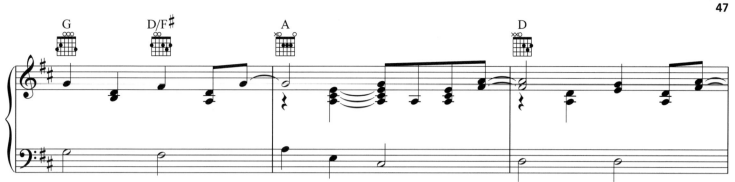

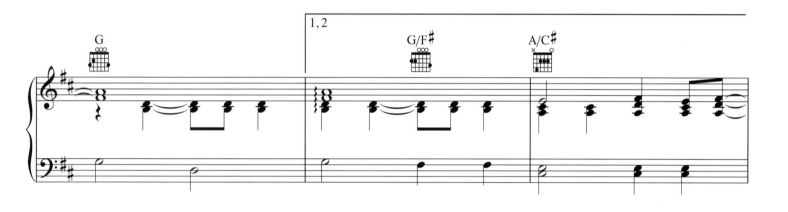

Yes, and

CHEVY VAN

Words and Music by
SAMMY JOHNS

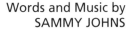

Relaxed

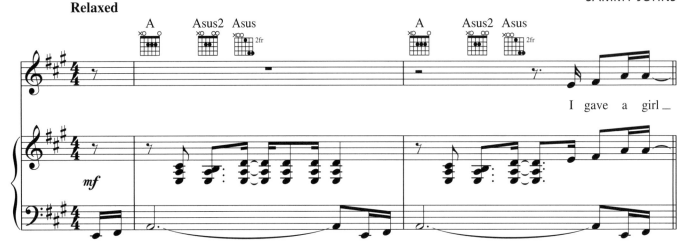

I gave a girl ___

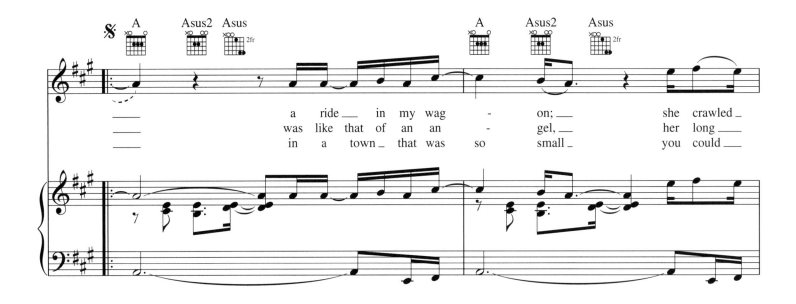

___ a ride ___ in my wag - on; ___ she crawled ___
___ was like that of an an - gel, ___ her long ___
___ in a town ___ that was so small ___ you could ___

in _____ and took ___ con - trol. ___ She was tired; ___
legs _____ were tanned ___ and brown. ___ Bet - ter keep ___
throw a rock from end to end. ___ A dirt road

as her mind___ was a - drag - ging,___ I said, "Get___
your eyes___ on the road, son.___ Bet - ter slow___
street, she walked off___ in___ bare feet.___ It's a shame___

___ some sleep___ and dream___ of rock and___ roll." _____
_____ this___ ve - hi - cle___ down. _____
___ I won't___ be pass - ing through___ a - gain. _____

'Cause like a pic - ture she was

To Coda ⊕

lay - ing there,___ moon - light danc - ing off her hair._____ She woke up___ and took me

by the hand. ___ She's gon-na love me in my ___ Chev-y van ___ and that's ___ al - right ___ with me. ___

Her young face ___

DEAD SKUNK

By LOUDON WAINWRIGHT III

DOCTOR, MY EYES

Words and Music by
JACKSON BROWNE

Repeat and Fade

DIMMING OF THE DAY

Written by
RICHARD THOMPSON

Moderate Country Ballad

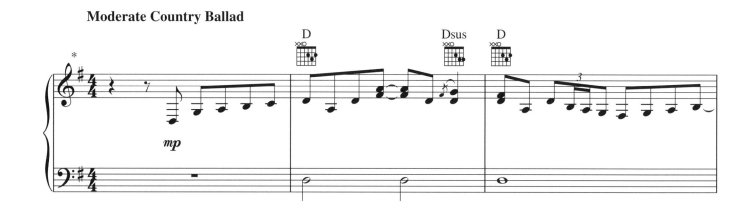

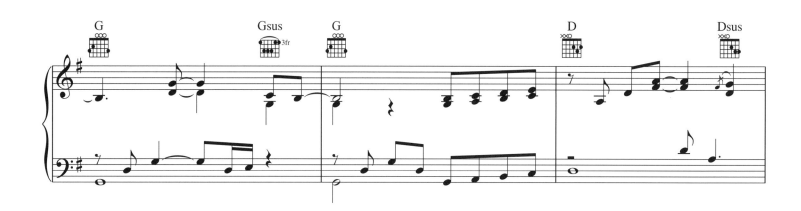

This old house _____ have come _____ is fall-ing down _____ a-round _____ my _____
_____ you to keep _____ us far _____ a-
on the street _____ in com - pa -

Recorded a half step higher.

D.S. al Coda

What days ___ I see ___

Yes, ___ I need you ___ at the

dim-ming of the day. ___

DO YOU WANNA MAKE LOVE

Words and Music by
PETER McCANN

Moderately fast

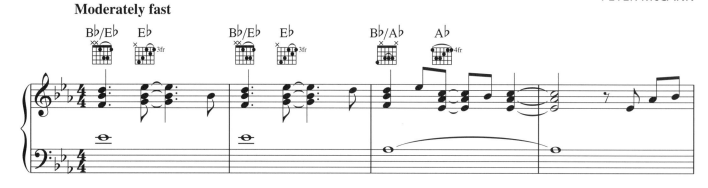

Some - times the love rhymes that fill the af - ter - noon
Take all the free - dom that a lov - er will al - low

lose all their mean - ing with the ris - ing moon.
if you feel the feel - ing that I'm feel - ing now.

EVERYBODY'S TALKIN'

(Echoes)

from MIDNIGHT COWBOY

Words and Music by
FRED NEIL

Lyrics under the staves:

Ev - ery - bod - y's talk - in' at me, I don't hear a

word they're say - in', on - ly the ech - oes of my

mind. Peo - ple

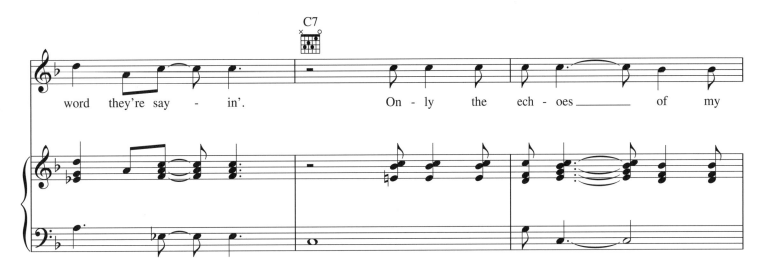

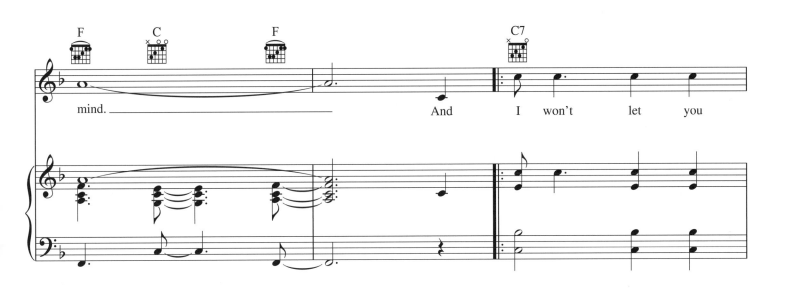

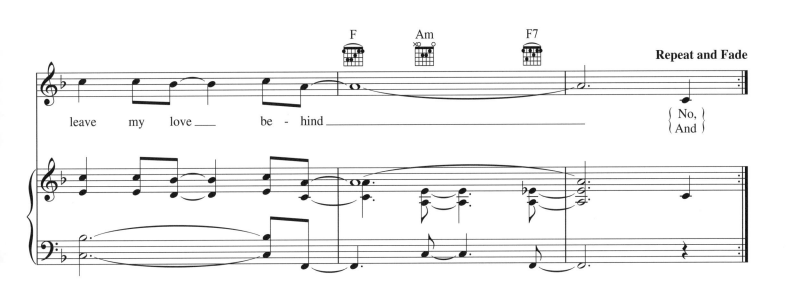

EVERYDAY I WRITE THE BOOK

Words and Music by
ELVIS COSTELLO

FAST CAR

Words and Music by
TRACY CHAPMAN

HELLO, IT'S ME

Words and Music by
TODD RUNDGREN

HELP ME MAKE IT THROUGH THE NIGHT

Words and Music by
KRIS KRISTOFFERSON

Moderately

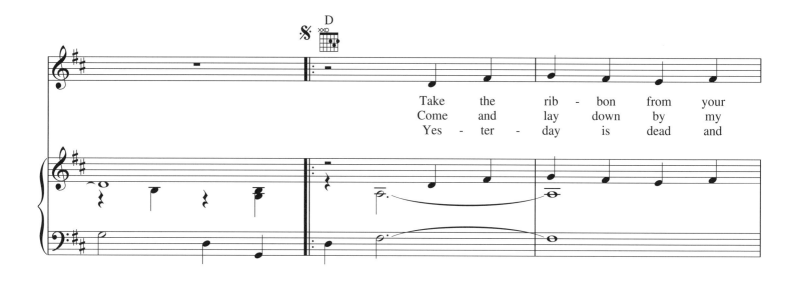

Take   the   rib - bon   from   your
Come   and   lay   down   by   my
Yes - ter - day   is   dead   and

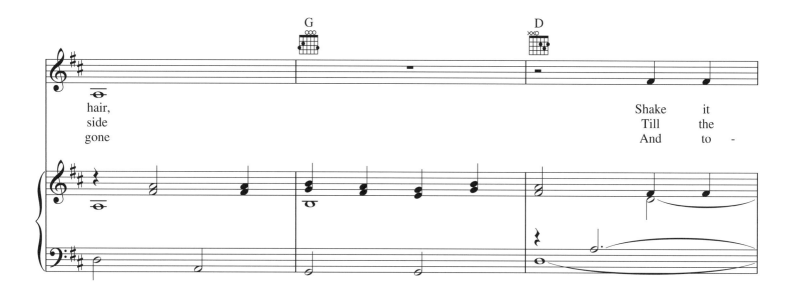

hair,
side
gone

Shake   it
Till   the
And   to -

I AIN'T MARCHING ANYMORE

Words and Music by
PHIL OCHS

Brightly

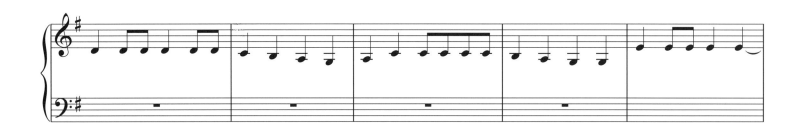

Oh, I marched to the Bat - tle of _____
stole Cal - i - for - nia from the
flew the fi - nal mis - sion in the

I GO CRAZY

Words and Music by
PAUL DAVIS

I'D LOVE YOU TO WANT ME

Words and Music by
LOBO

Easy rock

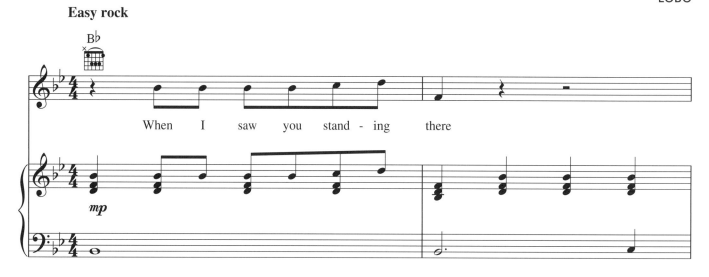

When I saw you stand-ing there

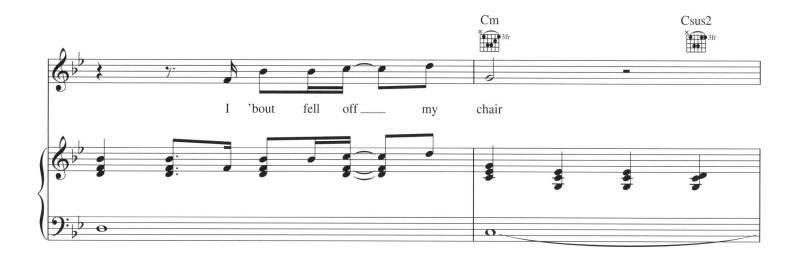

I 'bout fell off ___ my chair

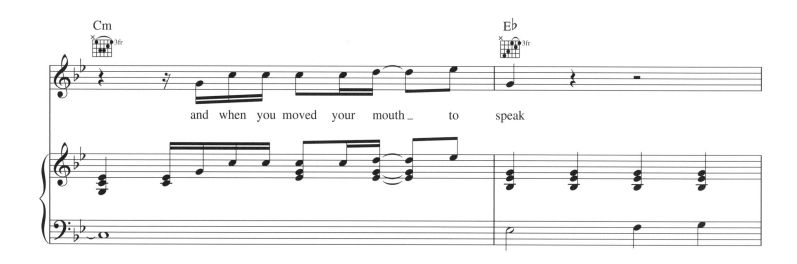

and when you moved your mouth ___ to speak

I'M IN YOU

Words and Music by
PETER FRAMPTON

I'm in you, ____ you're in me. __

I'm in you, _____

you're in me. _____ 'Cause you

gave me the love, _____ love that I nev-er had. _____

You gave me the love, _____ love that I nev - er had. _____

I don't care _____ where I go _____ when I'm

with _____ you.

rit.

I'M NOT IN LOVE

Words and Music by ERIC STEWART
and GRAHAM GOULDMAN

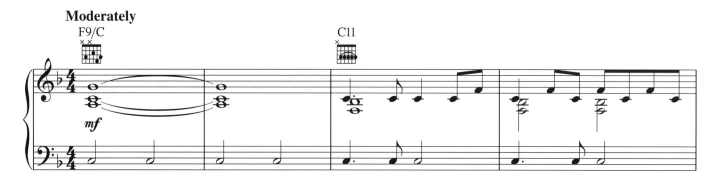

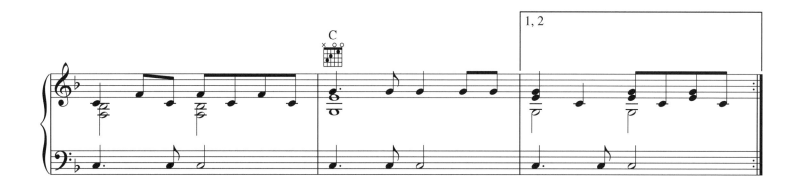

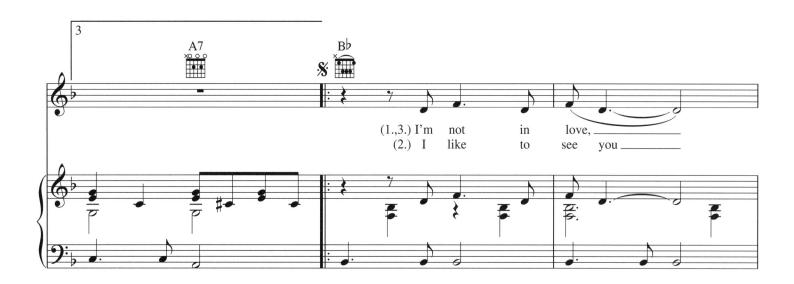

(1.,3.) I'm not in love, _____
(2.) I like to see you _____

Be quiet, big boys don't

IF I HAD A BOAT

Words and Music by
LYLE LOVETT

Country, with movement

IF I WERE A CARPENTER

Words and Music by
TIM HARDIN

If I ____ were a car - pen - ter, ____
If I ____ worked my hands in wood, _

and you were a la - dy, ____
would you still ____ love me?

would you mar - ry me
An - swer me, ____ babe,

123

IT'S A HARD LIFE WHEREVER YOU GO

Words and Music by
NANCI GRIFFITH

Additional Lyrics

2. Cafeteria line in Chicago;
   The fat man in front of me
   Is calling black people trash to his children,
   And he's the only trash here I see.
   And I'm thinking, this man wears a white hood
   In the night when his children should sleep;
   But they'll slip to their windows, and they'll see him,
   And they'll think that white hood's all they need.
   Chorus

3. I was a child in the Sixties,
   When dreams could be had through T.V.,
   With Disney and Cronkite and Martin Luther;
   And I believed, I believed, I believed.
   Now, I'm a back-seat driver from America,
   And I am not at the wheel of control,
   And I am guilty, and I am war, and I am the root of all evil,
   Lord, and I can't drive on the left side of the road.
   Chorus

IT'S TOO LATE

Words and Music by CAROLE KING
and TONI STERN

JACKIE BLUE

Words and Music by LARRY LEE
and STEVE CASH

Moderate rock ♩ = 100

Oo, _____
Oo, _____
Oo, _____

Jack - ie Blue   lives her life ___ from   in - side of a   room, ___
Jack - ie Blue,   what's a game, ___ girl,   if   you nev - er   lose? ___
Jack - ie Blue   likes a dream ___ that   can   nev - er come true. ___

*Recorded one whole step lower.

LAY DOWN
(Candles in the Rain)

Words and Music by
MELANIE SAFKA

Slow Gospel Rock

Lay down, lay down, lay it all down, let your white birds smile up at the ones who stand __ and frown. Lay down, lay down, lay it all down, let your white birds smile up at the ones who stand __ and frown.

D

We were so close, _____ there was no room, **Em**

We bled in-

D

side _____ each oth-er's wounds. **Em**

We all had **D**

caught _____ the same dis-

Em

ease, and we all **D**

sang _____ the songs of **To Coda** ⊕ **Em**

peace. _____

G

Lay down, **D**

lay down, **F**

lay it all down, **G**

let your

JESSIE

Words and Music by
JOSHUA KADISON

LEAVE ME ALONE
(Ruby Red Dress)

Words and Music by
LINDA LAURIE

MY MARIA

Words and Music by DANIEL J. MOORE
and B.W. STEVENSON

My Ma - ri - a,
- a,

don't you know ___ I've come a long, long way? ___
there were some blue and sor - rowed times. ___

I've been long - in' to see _____ her. When ___ she's a - round, _
Just my thoughts ___ a - bout _____ you bring ___ back

LONGER

Words and Music by
DAN FOGELBERG

I'll be in love __ with you. __

Long-er than __ there've been

MAGNET AND STEEL

Words and Music by
WALTER LINDSAY EGAN

ME AND JULIO DOWN BY THE SCHOOLYARD

Words and Music by
PAUL SIMON

1. The Ma-ma py-ja-ma rolled out-ta bed and she ran to the po-lice sta-

Whistle

D.S. al Coda

2. Whoa, _ in a

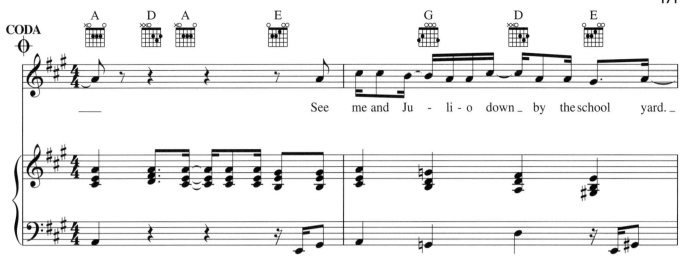

See me and Ju - li - o down by the school yard.

Repeat ad lib. to fade

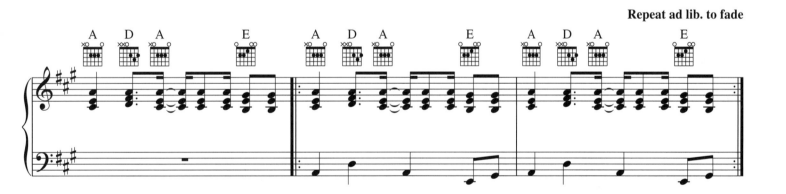

Additional Lyrics

3. In a couple of days they come and take me away
But the press let their story leak
And when the radical Priest come to get me released
We was all on the cover of Newsweek.

And I'm on my way *etc.*

OL' 55

Words and Music by
TOM WAITS

Lord, ___ don't you know ___ the feel - in's get - tin' strong - er ___

Well, my

D.S. al Coda

CODA

Free - way cars and trucks. ___

Repeat and Fade

rid - in' with La - dy Luck, ___

POETRY MAN

Words and Music by
PHOEBE SNOW

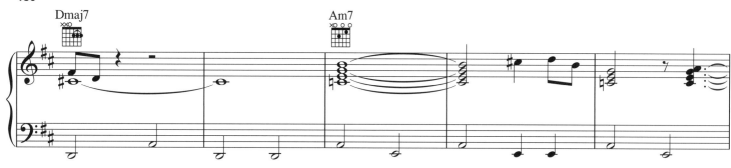

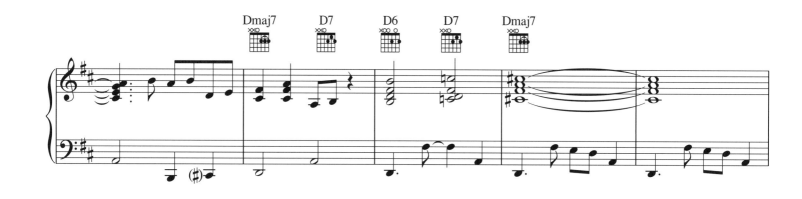

Talk ___ to me some more. You don't have to go. ___ You're the

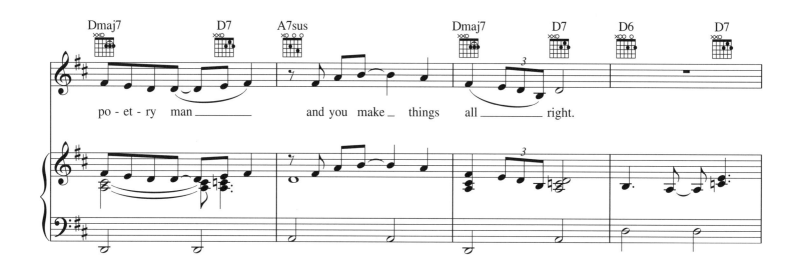

po - et - ry man ___ and you make ___ things all ___ right.

ON AND ON

Words and Music by
STEPHEN BISHOP

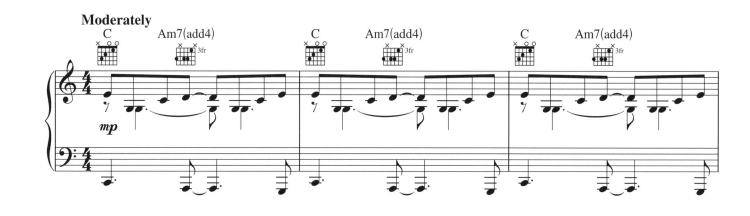

Down in Ja - mai - ca they got lots of pret - ty wom - en.
Poor ol' Jim - my sits a - lone in the moon - light.
sun on my shoul - ders and my toes in the sand.

Steal your mon - ey, then they break your heart. Lone - some Sue, she's in
Saw his wom - an kiss an - oth - er man. So he takes a lad - der; steals the
Wom - an's left me for some oth - er man. Ah, but I don't care. I'll just

PANCHO AND LEFTY

Written by
TOWNES VAN ZANDT

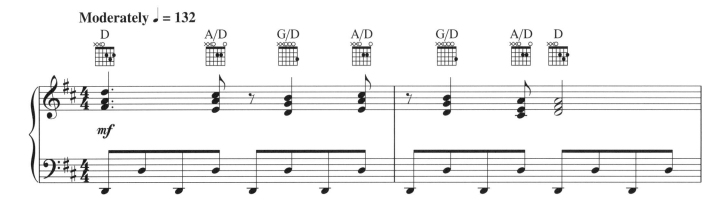

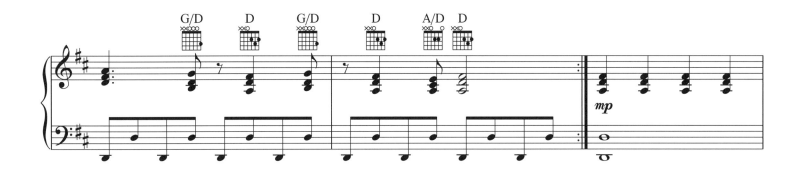

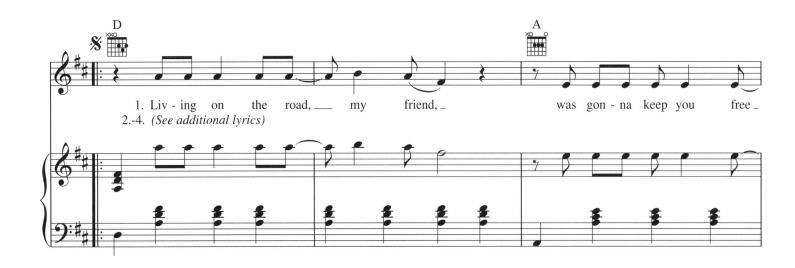

1. Liv-ing on the road, ___ my friend, ___ was gon-na keep you free ___

2.-4. *(See additional lyrics)*

D.S. (3rd verse)
D.S.S. (Instr.)
D.S. (4th verse)
D.S.S. al Coda

out of kind - ness I___ sup - pose.

CODA

pose.

Additional Lyrics

2. Pancho was a bandit boy,
   His horse was fast as polished steel.
   He wore his gun outside his pants,
   For all the honest world to feel.
   Well, Pancho met his match, you know,
   On the deserts down in Mexico.
   Nobody heard his dying word,
   Ah, but that's the way it goes.

3. Lefty, he can't sing the blues,
   All night long like he used to.
   The dust that Pancho bit down south,
   Ended up in Lefty's mouth.
   The day they laid poor Pancho low,
   Lefty split for Ohio.
   Where he got the bread to go,
   There ain't nobody know.

4. The poet's tell how Pancho felt,
   And Lefty's living in a cheap hotel;
   The desert's quiet, and Cleveland's cold,
   And so the story ends we're told.
   Pancho needs your prayers, it's true,
   And save a few for Lefty, too.
   He only did what he had to do,
   And now, he's growing old.

PEACE TRAIN

Words and Music by
CAT STEVENS

-in' late-ly ____ think-in' a-bout the good things ____ to come.

and I ____ be-lieve _____ it could ____ be. Some-thing ____ good

has be-gun. Oh, peace train ____ sound - in' loud - er.

glide on ____ the peace train.

PRECIOUS AND FEW

Words and Music by
WALTER D. NIMS

REASON TO BELIEVE

Words and Music by
TIM HARDIN

TAKE A LETTER, MARIA

Words and Music by
R. B. GREAVES

Additional Lyrics

2. You've been many things, but most of all a secretary to me,
   And it's times like this I feel you've always been close to me.
   Was I wrong to work nights to try to build a good life?
   All work and no play has just cost me a wife.
   (Chorus:)

3. When a man loves a woman, it's hard to understand
   That she would find more pleasure in the arms of another man.
   I never really noticed how sweet you are to me,
   It just so happens I'm free tonight, would you like to have dinner with me?
   (Chorus:)

ROMEO'S TUNE

Words and Music by
STEVE FORBERT

Moderate pop rock

Meet _ me in the mid-dle of the day, _ let me hear you say _ ev-'ry-thing's _ o-kay, _

{ bring me _ south-ern kiss-es from _ your room. _
{ come on _ out be-neath the shin - ing sun. _

SAD EYES

Words and Music by
ROBERT JOHN PEDRICK

SAN FRANCISCO
(Be Sure to Wear Some Flowers in Your Hair)

Words and Music by
JOHN PHILLIPS

A SONG FOR YOU

Words and Music by
LEON RUSSELL

Slowly

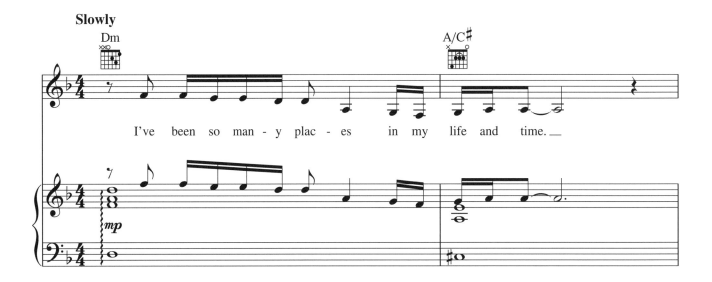

I've been so man-y plac-es in my life and time. __

I've sung a lot of songs, __ I've made some bad rhyme. I've

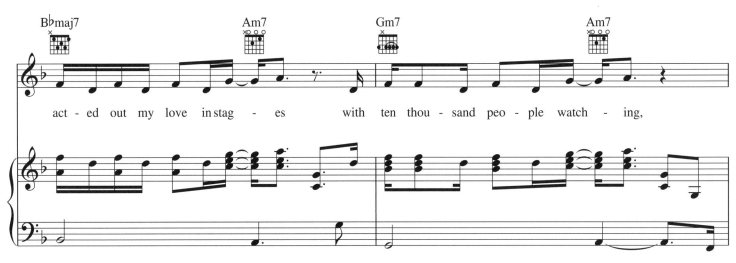

act-ed out my love in stag-es with ten thou-sand peo-ple watch-ing,

lis - ten to the mel - o - dy, __ 'cause my love is in there hid - ing.

I love you in a place where there's no space or time. __ I

love you for my life; _____ you are a friend of mine. __ And

D.S. al Coda

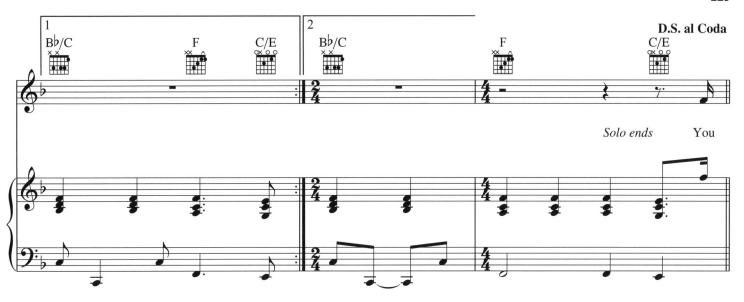

Solo ends   You

We were a - lone and I was sing - ing this song __ for you. __

We were a - lone and I was sing - ing this song _____ for you.

STREETS OF LONDON

Words and Music by
RALPH McTELL

Moderately fast

mind.

mind.

Additional Lyrics

3. In the all night café at a quarter past eleven,
   Same old man sitting there on his own.
   Looking at the world over the rim of his teacup,
   Each tea lasts an hour and he wanders home alone.

4. Have you seen the old man outside the seaman's mission,
   Memory fading with the medal ribbons that he wears?
   In our winter city the rain cries a little pity
   For one more forgotten hero and a world that doesn't care.

SUZANNE

Words and Music by
LEONARD COHEN

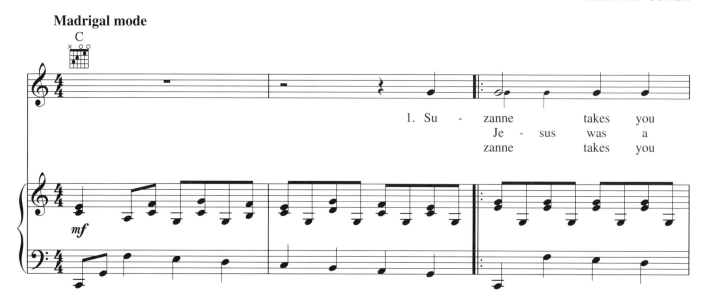

TEACH YOUR CHILDREN

Words and Music by
GRAHAM NASH

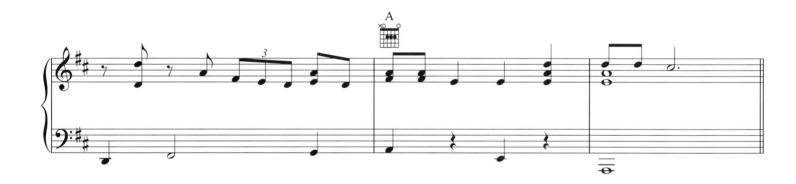

You   who are on the road ____

Teach   your chil - dren
Teach   your par - ents

well;   their fa - ther's hell
well;   their chil - dren's hell

did slow - ly go _____ by. _____
will slow - ly go _____ by. _____
    And

feed   then on ____ your dreams,

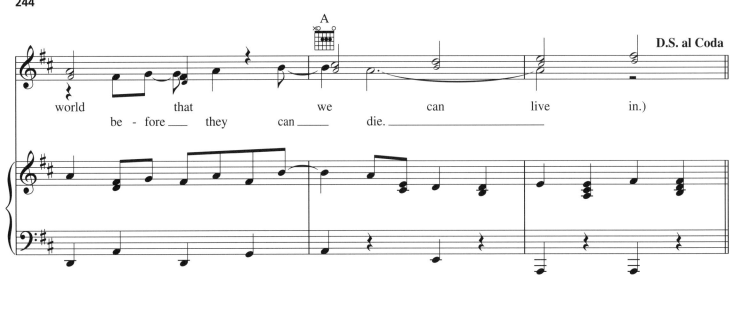

world   that   we   can   live   in.)
be - fore ___ they   can ___   die. _____

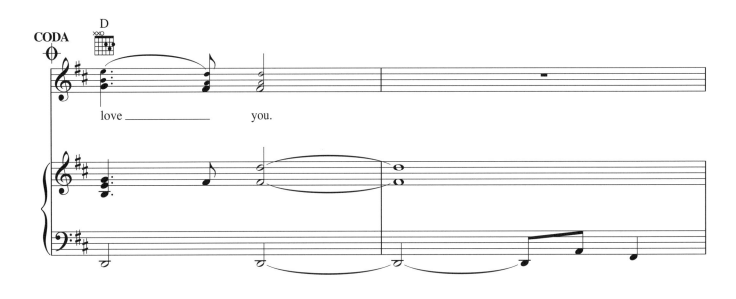

love _____   you.

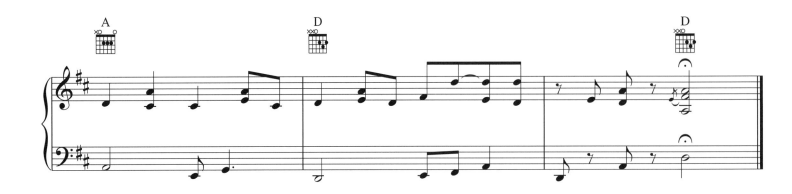

WHAT HAVE THEY DONE TO MY SONG, MA?

Words and Music by
MELANIE SAFKA

Play 8 times

1. Look what they've done _ to _ my song, _____ Ma. _
2. Look what they've done _ to _ my brain, _____ Ma. _
3. I wish I could find _ a _ good book _ to live in.

4-8. see additional lyrics

Look what they've done to my song. _
Look what they've done to my brain. _
Wish I could find a good book. _

Well it's the
Well they _
Well if _

on - ly thing _ I can do al - right _ and they turned it up - side down, oh Ma,

look _ what they've done _ to my song. _ song.

Repeat and Fade

Optional Ending

Additional lyrics

4. La da da da...
   Look what they've done to my song

5. Maybe it'll all be alright, Ma
   Maybe it'll all be okay
   Well if the people are buying tears
   I'll be rich some day, Ma
   Look what they've done to my song

6. Ils ont change ma chanson ma
   Ils ont change ma chanson
   C'est la seule chose que je peuz faire
   Et ce n'est pas bon ma
   Ils ont change ma chanson.

7. Look what they've done to my song, Ma
   Look what they've done to my song, Ma
   Well they tied it in a plastic bag
   And they turned it upside down, Ma
   Look what they've done to my song

8. Ils ont change ma chanson ma
   Ils ont change ma chanson
   C'est la seule chose que je peuz faire
   Et ce n'est pas bon ma
   Ils ont change ma chanson.

WAVELENGTH

Words and Music by
VAN MORRISON

WE JUST DISAGREE

Words and Music by
JIM KRUEGER

YEAR OF THE CAT

Words and Music by IAN ALASTIR STEWART
and PETER WOOD

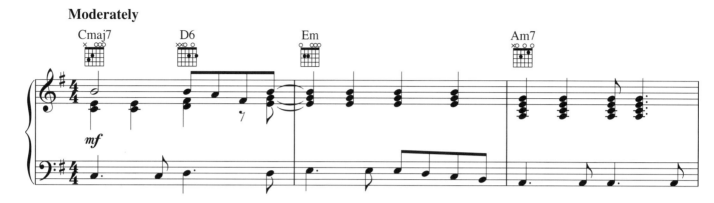

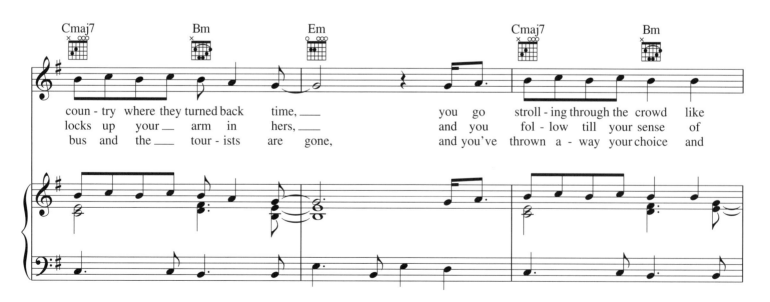

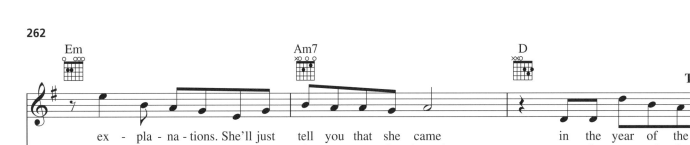

To Coda ⊕

ex - pla - na - tions. She'll just tell you that she came in the year of the cat. _
feel my life just like a riv - er run - ning through the year of the cat." _
bound to leave her, but for now you're gon - na stay in the year of the cat. _

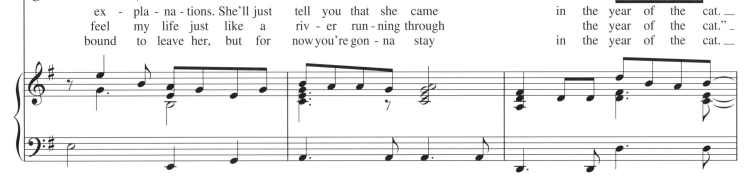

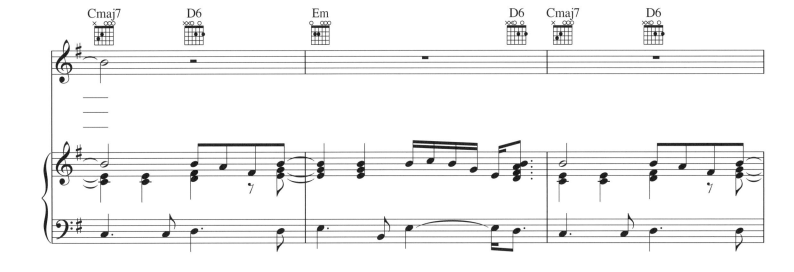

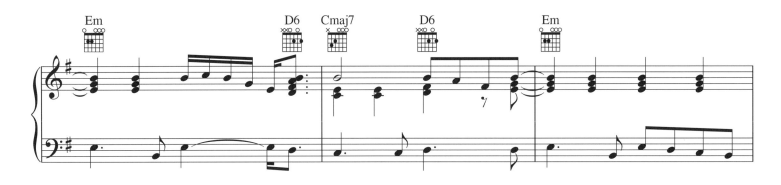

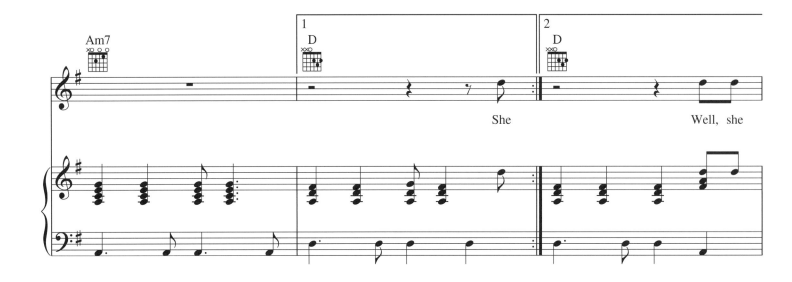

She

Well, she

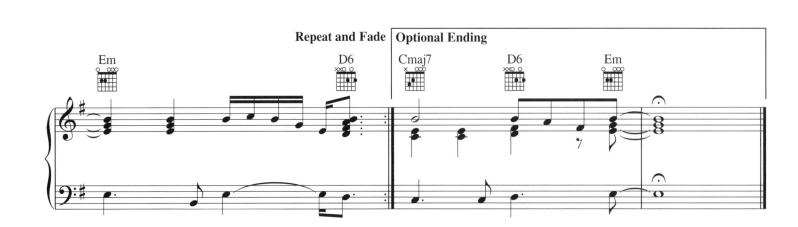

YOU'RE ONLY LONELY

Words and Music by
JOHN DAVID SOUTHER

YOU'VE GOT A FRIEND

Words and Music by
CAROLE KING

*Vocal harmony sung 2nd time only

YOUR SONG

Words and Music by ELTON JOHN
and BERNIE TAUPIN

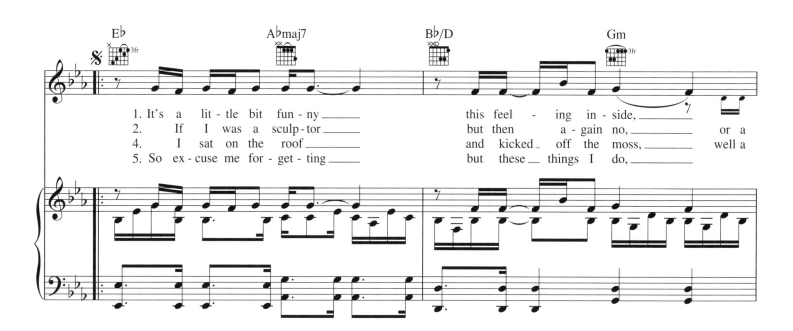

1. It's a lit-tle bit fun-ny _____ this feel-ing in-side, _____
2. If I was a sculp-tor _____ but then a-gain no, _____ or a
4. I sat on the roof _____ and kicked off the moss, _____ well a
5. So ex-cuse me for-get-ting _____ but these things I do, _____

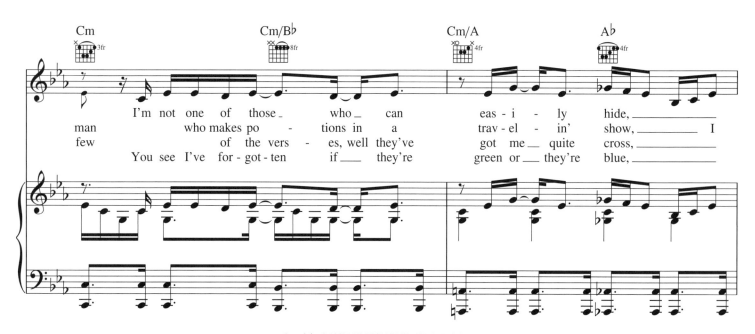

I'm not one of those who can eas-i-ly hide, _____
man who makes po-tions in a trav-el-in' show, _____ I
few of the vers-es, well they've got me quite cross, _____ I
You see I've for-got-ten if they're green or they're blue, _____

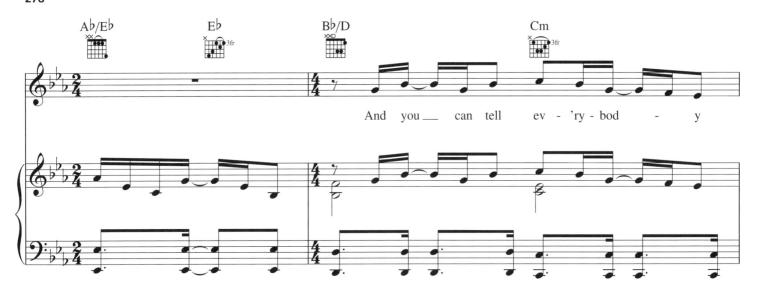

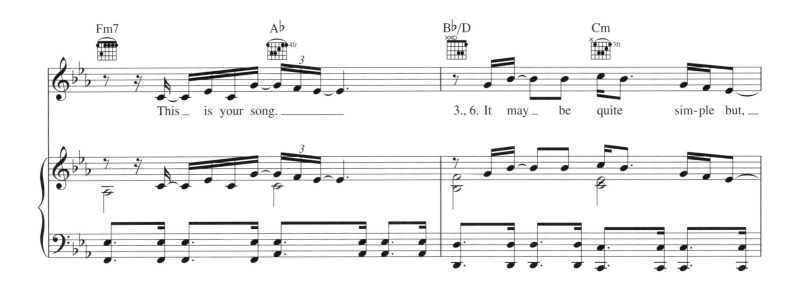

that I put down in words. How won-der-ful life is while

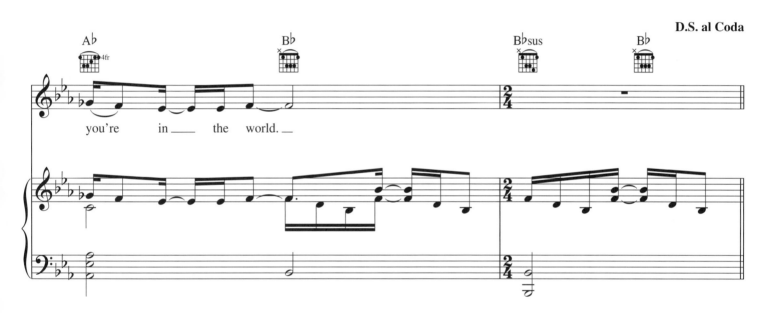

D.S. al Coda

you're in the world.

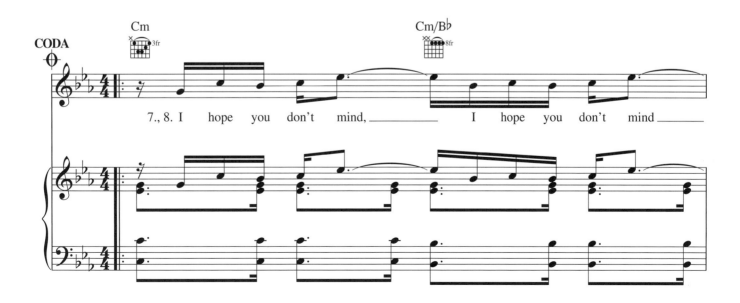

CODA

7., 8. I hope you don't mind, I hope you don't mind

that I put down in words, How won-der-ful life is while

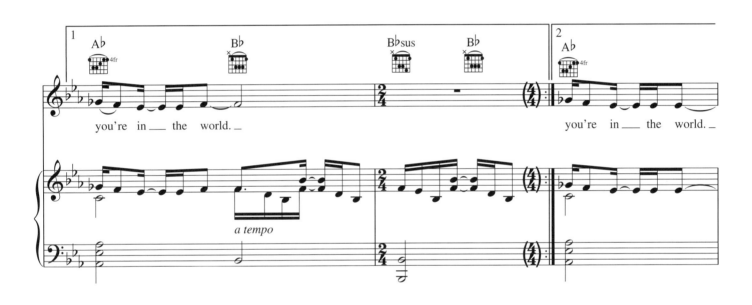

you're in the world. you're in the world.

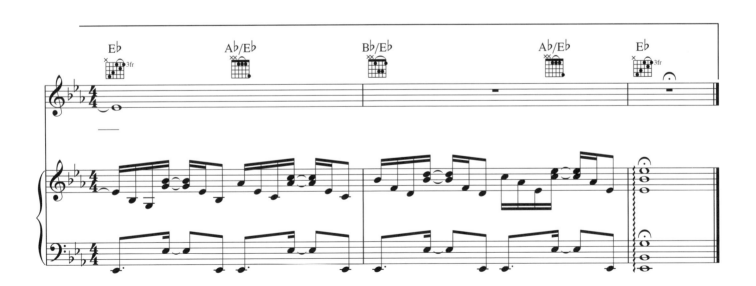